# Magnus is Stuck

by Tim Little

Illustrated by Bill Ledger

OXFORD
UNIVERSITY PRESS

Pip

Pip can pick up rocks.

Magnus

Magnus picks up a sack.

A gust picks up Magnus!

Magnus is stuck.

Pip runs to get a rock.

Pip gets on the rock.

Pip spins it.

Pip gets Magnus.

# Retell the story ...

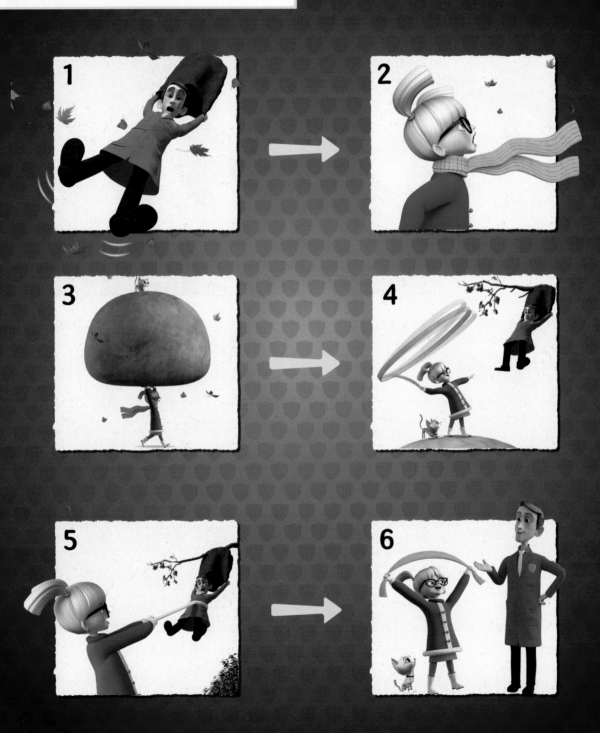